To Kelly and

Delia!

THE POWER

OF HEALING POETRY

Delia B. Freinquel

Essential Consulting Studio

Library of Congress Catalog Card Number: 98-93487

The Power of Healing Poetry
Written and Illustrated by Delia B. Freinquel

Copyright © 1998, by Delia B. Freinquel

All rights reserved. No part of this book may be
reproduced or transmitted in any manner, without
the prior permission in writing from the author.

Published by Essential Consulting Studio
1295 Beacon St. P.O.Box 733
Brookline - MA - 02446-0006

ISBN 0-9665872-0-0

Printed and bound in the United States of America

This edition first published 1998

Contents

VI

INTRODUCTION

My poems are about love, happiness, power,
peace, war, healing, food, pain, relief, justice,
God, loneliness, religion, eternity, legacy,
nature, life, death, and fame.
The words have been carefully chosen
for their excellence.
My poetry supports the healing through
alternative medicine and spirituality, and
the purpose is to heal:
words sometimes have more power than
medicine.
A poem is a verse composition with rhythm
and intense emotional tone, characterized by
beauty and creative power.
My poems express my feelings, and I crafted
them with art and sensibility.

Delia B. Freinquel

FAME

Fame is all about a name,
Smile of pearls
Carmine lips
Silk and velvet tight fit dress.
Diamonds and gold
Envy her splendor,
Adored by millions will shine forever.
Form and style
And famous headlines,
Now she lies between the stars.
Her love belongs to others
Glitter in the highest,
Praised her so huge.
She will come back
To the ones she loves,
No longer young and coming of age
There are no more famous days,
The time belongs to others.
She will cry in despair,
Oh, those famous days!
But soft will grow in her
The time of resignation.
One day her life story she may write,
To start again the road of fame.

HAPPINESS

I came that day so clear
To live in that house near.
I feel sometimes at the top of the hill,
Or surfing at high speed in the rill.

Again I walk alone the shore
Only just once more,
When winter comes
Summer becomes
In sweet remembrances,
In times of happiness.

A message I will send
To my best friend,
I feel something very deep,
I would love forever to keep.

I will tell
To my friend I am feeling well
And I do not my friend cheat
With a lie maybe sweet.
I believe it is happiness indeed
And really this is all that I need.

WALKING THE BEACH

My poem has the color of tenderness
With golden sand and blooming trees,
People of the long shore
Walking all along and more,
Proud they go men and women alone
Like the seagulls flying their own.

The picture there
Perfect was everywhere,
While the waves white and blue steam
Are coming from the sea like a dream.
Sweet purple shell so dear
I will keep it up there.

Soft, it lasts long
The foam in the shore along,
A good positive feeling of calm
The walk has been like a balm,
Loving the joy like a magic touch
I have for the day too much.

THE SOUP OF EVERY DAY

Seaweed from deep sea water
Warms my spirit and my whole being.
Smooth and plenty of colors,
Orange for carrots,
Green for spinach,
White for onions,
And beige ginger roots.
I have nature in my dish,
Where my soup sits.
Exquisite beyond words
With a blessing broth
So warm, so filling.
My silver spoon
With my name written in the handle,
Is ready to be used
To have my golden soup.
The luck of goodness
To dine at this sacred table.
The pleasure inside
And a feeling of comfort
Now belong to me.

MY TULIP

My tulip has a loving care
And the color of beauty.
Single and lonely,
It waits for daylight.

My tulip is gracious
And will last forever.
It is shaped perfectly,
In just a piece of clay.

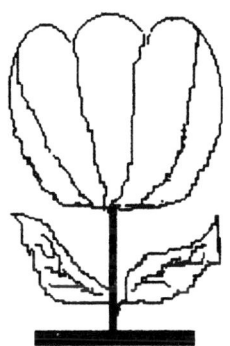

MY WISH TO GOD

When my time is up,
Make my road easy.
I will honor you
With my lyrical songs.

I will reach an altar,
I will pray in the name
Of all religions,
Of all human beings.

When my time is up,
I will be alone
With my compassion,
With no desperation.

With all the goodness,
With all the strength,
I will walk your path
To your kingdom of wisdom.

When my time is up,
I will love your throne divine,
I will be blessed with grace,
I will live in your sacred house.

FLOWER I

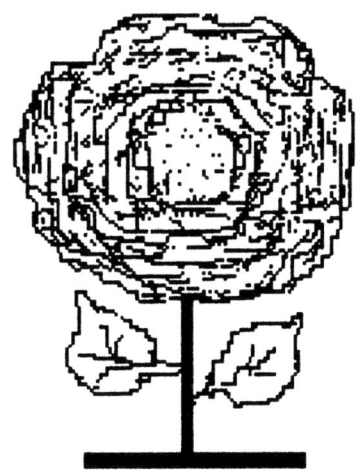

THE SPIRITUAL CLASS

My spiritual day has begun even
With meditation time given,
A relaxing feeling arises
By the time I open my eyes.

I feel I was visiting
A far land truly exciting,
Castles where I have been before,
A land with golden sand and more.

With healing relief from pain
I would love to try this discipline again.
The music started triumphal
From ancient wisdom patriarchal.

A time to relax I share
With myself and I do care.
I have chosen a secret word,
The word which belongs to my private world.

I sent to my universe
This enchanted verse,
The symbol is concentration I preach
This is what I want to teach.

DELIGHTED WITH MY RECIPES

In culinary art I have been educated
With joy my time to cook I have been dedicated,
So, I will start
With some ingredients apart.

I will measure the flour,
Add my natural cream sour,
And some herbs which I have grown
In the garden on my own.

The oven is cooking my bread just plain
As I taste a simple grain,
The music is in the air by chance
As I start a dance.

That I have always good humor
Is between my friends a rumor,
To cook for me is a recreation
With a healing dance and meditation.

A blue sky without clouds and still bare
With a warm breeze in the air,
I can for a while rest
Before greeting my guest.

BEYOND THERE

I will live in the eternal
Silence of tomorrow.
Neither the heaven
Nor the sky
Will see me again.

The landscape will keep quiet
And lonely.
Days or nights,
The time does not exist.

The house will be in permanent solitude.
The sorrow and the grief,
Will be there
As an expression of love.
Remembrances from old times,
Will fill the rooms,
The space, and the walls of the house.

IT WILL ALWAYS BELONG TO ME

He is not here anymore;
A warm day became a cold night
And I feel lonely again.

It has been a long time,
Since love filled my soul.

It has been a long time,
Since I have had that feeling.

A sweet, fond remembrance
Will always belong to me.

PREDICTED

It was a real explanation,
Only success was the definition,
It comes, as always so clear,
The prophecy was near.

A fortuneteller predicted:
"To love you will be addicted"
As you are very emancipated,
The family charm incarnated,
With certain rich roots
And a great confidence.

FLOWER II

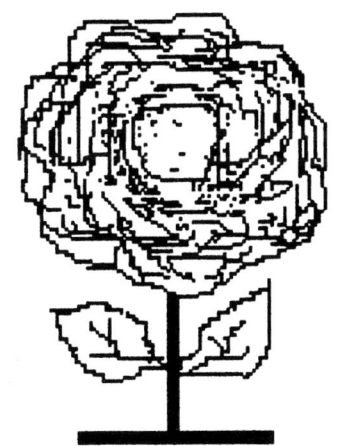

AT EVENING

When day becames night,
Evening leans in a starry heaven.

It is time for a gloaming prayer,
The sun hidden behind a deep blue hill.

While the mountains hold the gold,
The skyey, so marvelous to contemplate.

A pale moonlight,
Soothing in secret the flowers dew.

The wind softly brings the fruit's scents,
My joy goes whither it can reach.

WISH

The return to calm,
Sparse the spiritual condition.

The quality of commodities,
The most precious belongings.

The Creation is to be preserved
With simple things as instant gratification.

MY MOUNTAINS

My mountains: a lonely world,
A place to heal the soul.
My mountains: form, texture
And perfect grace.
I can feel the great majesty
And reflect and love
That moment of peace.
Stillness in the air
As I sit on a millenary stone.
A herd far and running
Through the rugged ground lea.
The place is a blessing,
A moment's lull.
What a wonder the sun,
Warming the morning.
The hamlet wakes up to a new day.
My mountains change colors,
And so the spot of still water.
My mountains: challenge and creation.

THE LADY IN BLUE

The lady in blue my neighbor,
They said she was a woman of power,
Happens to be the master of ceremonies,
Still kind and generous,
Still a singular style.

In a warm and friendly note,
To her party I was invited.
The lady in blue was waiting,
To greet the newcomers,
And to talk about natural life.

She comes from a prominent family;
Every corner of the house was richness,
Things so precise and many amenities
A liberal expression of a fashionable look,
The house was her retreat.

The lady in blue talked
With remarkable understanding
Of human nature,
Between shining porcelain and tea,
The ecstasy was in every soul.

THE AUDITION

Silent and waiting,
Ready for training.
When a time of audition comes
In all excitement my life becomes.
And suddenly I am playing a Greek God, the last.
In my imagination it happens so fast.
At that point to reality I reach
My coach ready for me to teach.
So I get into the net
And all for me was set.
This is the world in which I belong.
I became secure and strong,
Just a great similitude
With the biggest stars' attitude.
None came to me to protect,
Alone I gave my audition as I expect.
I am already in the cast
It happened so fast.
There for me was the sun,
My new life has just begun.

FLOWER III

TALK TO ME

Talk to me

About pain, if you need relief.

About happiness, if you want to share.

About secrets, if you need to hide.

About freedom, if you feel like flying.

About the moon and the stars, if you are in love.

About life, if you feel the joy of being alive.

About death, if your time is short enough.

About eternity, if your name will shine forever.

About a long journey, if you have a story to tell.

THE DANCER

Born to dance crowded theaters,
Dancing the music of the masters.
The supreme power of movement,
Success the first announcement.

Dressed in silk a swan she tries,
What a pleasure for the eyes.
Such a wonder everywhere,
The expression of art was there.

I wish myself dancing to glory,
Possessed like her without a worry.
A time of triumph I desire,
Forward to combine what I admire.

Beyond ambition, blooming
Flowers to honor the dancer raising.
The star's new time will begin
Happiness and mirth within.

MY FLOWERS

I wake up,
Spring is in my house.
I water my flowers
In the morning.
They will be kissed by sunlight
During day time.
For them I will turn on a light
In the evening.
When winter comes
For months it will last,
I will take care of my flowers
As I did in the past.
It will be nice,
To save them from the snow and the ice.
They will bloom into beauty,
They will bring gaiety
They will bring peace,
In soft colors and ease.

DESERT PLANTS

You are mortal
You will not live eternally
Like desert plants
They will bury your bones.

Unique stems
Purple and green colors,
Hard and proud
Without love and fondness.

The rain from heaven
Is their blessing water.
Lonely landscape of desert plants.

THE LONELY

The years to come
Be always in touch with yourself,
Unto the last day of your life.
Enjoy your own company,
At the end of all
You are the only one you will have.
You will continue the road alone,
That will be your temple.
Where you live and rest,
Where you stay and pray,
When you have to be brave and wise,
When you are in pain or need relief,
When you spare your time,
Or take your time alone.
When you delight and have joy,
Or when you weep or have sorrow.
Clear your spirit,
Live your days with intensity,
Look forward to love,
And kindly take destiny with glory,
The years to come.

DESTINY

Written like a story I have to play
It says all about my way.
If I will live long
If I will be strong
If I will live with vanity
If I will live with modesty.
All was written
All was chosen.
I have to walk the road
The written path by God,
Without any supplication
With no chance of explanation.
Lines will not be changed
This is my life with tomorrows
Written for me without any sorrows,
It says that I will have a lot of glory
And merry seasons filled with plenty of poetry.

THE ADVICE

It is something I want you to say
And it is not about your way,
I simply want you to stay
And if you listen, I will cheer with a prayer.

Wisdom runs in my family
We are great advisors naturally,
With good soul religiously
And good experience previously.

Advice is always a wisdom collection,
If you follow the rules without exception,
And please do not believe this is a private invasion,
It is just to warn you about deception.

It is a belief that advice has no price.
Then I hope that you are not surprised,
If to be old means to be wise,
It is an old tradition in my family to advise.

Please accept the advice I give you with modesty,
It represents the family for a dynasty,
It will teach you to go through life with generosity,
And have an existence shaped in honesty.

THE PHILOSOPHY OF POSITIVISM

Feeling infinite delight that evening
I read widely the books I decided to bring.
My vacation time and my privacy
Are important forms of secrecy.

My personal interest in happiness
Encourage me to defy dreariness,
So happiness is the result of positivism
A condition you can reach if you start with optimism.

The road is not easy to achieve
But can be easy as far as you believe.
You don't need to be bold
This is what I was told.

It is important confidence,
Having vigor and self-assurance.
I start exploring positivism passionately;
The purpose is praiseworthy.

As soon as positivism is a conquest
You will feel at your best,
Everything going onward
And for trying hard, the reward.

BY MY OWN

I came to prove my luck
Along the road of life,
My songs of love
Give me strength and pride.
I will take the space,
I will be the first
Passing by my own.

The highest
I will reach
With my preaching.
To find happiness will become true
In despite of all
I have to go through.

Between my reality and my dream
I am following a gleam,
I will reach the top of the mountains
Look at the skies
And deeply love what I have,
In front of my eyes
With gratitude.

HERBS, A BLESSING FROM HEAVEN

Studies have shown
The great power by their own,
Always my herbs I carry
When I need them, I hurry.
This is the best way to be healthy,
It is more important than being wealthy.
Sweet or bitter herbs are my adoration,
It is a wise medicine, hence my explanation.

They have an ancient history,
Their roots are not a mystery,
Have them natural
And you will feel spiritual.
So feeling better,
The well-being will last longer,
Herbs take a time to go into action,
But the healing is a good sensation.

Health worth more than gold,
Have a blessing herb you will be told,
Health has no price,
Have herbal treatment for a strong rise.
God has created this wonder
For you to be healthier,
Put the herbs on the shelf,
And when you need them, help yourself.

MAGIC IN THE SEASON

The season when all is in bloom
The sun is in my room.

I can overlook the trees, I sing
To celebrate the beginning of the Spring.

The tulips lean over my garden pathway
In deep red and blue, they spread all the way.

I arrange the flowers always the same,
They are so pretty and so are their names.

Magic in the season
Magic in my being.

DINING ALONE

After a long journey, here I come.
What a relief to reach home,
It was a wonderful fair evening
A day for special giving.

And now the most important duty,
To set my table with plenty of beauty,
This is my sphere of action,
I love perfection.

Now without the stress,
I will choose my best dress
And I will receive from God
A positive nod.

I don't have to implore
To have at my table what I adore,
I have everything from the store
I bought for my dinner before.

This is what I call liberty
To cook just my specialty,
Blessing my table I discover
For dinner time I am a great lover.

BEAUTY IS IN HERE

It is beauty in green
The splendor I have seen,
Here and everywhere
The green, the grass, and the trees over there.

Maybe beauty is in blue,
And it is the real truth.
Such a perfect sight,
From the sun comes the light.

I can see beauty in fame,
I would love to have a famous name.
Or I should be on the stage,
Despite my age.

Maybe beauty is in the show,
Or in something that I bestow.
I use beauty like strength,
It is here all the way, all the length.

FLOWER IV

THE IMMIGRANT

The dream, a new land,
The work will be in the ground,
He becomes the group leader
Settling down as a rancher.

He won his life chance
And learned how to take the place,
A lot of good producing
A new language studying.

Labor his positive light,
Work to be rich he was right,
He creates a big corporation
Having great determination.

The best influence
Was his source,
Training was his decision
Without abdication.

Strong-willed, winner nominated
The immigrant craved,
After times with prosperity
Age, long life with dignity.

HERBS FROM THE MOUNTAINS

Early that morning I learned to my delight,
A friend from past years will stay overnight.
I went to the mountains as I wish,
To pick up some herbs for a delicious dish.

Up there the view was magnificent,
It was a pleasure, the green herb's scent.
The far crags look like a dream,
To reach one day that gleam.

A June sky blue my delight,
They said it will rain, it might.
Herbs to my friends I use to send,
It was a good time to spend.

They are the best
Fresh, tender, the loveliest.
A healthy way to honor my friend that evening,
Herbs from the mountains and even songs playing.

I sprinkle them with fresh water for freshness,
I treat my herbs with caresses.
It was a lovely dinner I can tell,
Herbs with healing virtues to be well.

MEET ME AT MY WINDOW

You have flown a long way
A silent flight in a deep sky,
Through sunny days or rain
You came from far away.
Here our mountains
Still crowned in white,
After a long cold winter
Sunlight is at my window.
Little bird sweet companion
Dressed in red, yellow, and blue.
The village wakes up
To your sweet song,
Little bird come to me,
Moving your wings with grace
In sparkling waves.
I will cherish you
I will pamper you.
Sing for me your song of love,
Sing for me your song of joy,
Come back next Spring,
Meet me at my window.

THE PRAYER

I am praying today,
Wishing my prayer
Gives you the power
And relief to recover.

May tomorrow be fair,
May peace be in the air,
Sky will be clear in all the countries,
People praying in the prairies.

My universal prayer is a must,
Life passes so fast,
An afternoon to care,
Lots of love to share.

A prayer for the poor and the rich,
All over I preach,
I promise a message will be sent,
And not in vain my time I spent.

A prayer for wisdom and joy,
And all the beauty in life you can enjoy,
I will fill my expectation,
Giving you consolation.

A TRIP, A DESTINY

A sparkling blue and white sky,
Me flying again to delight myself,
Art and beauty my destiny.
The temple of fashion,
A glimpse to other times, my option.
The gracious living and the magical,
Other centuries, and the masters,
Waiting for me.
The early important years,
And all of a sudden Paris,
With the charm,
With the beauty,
With the magnificence,
With lights and the reality,
Of a marvelous time
Eternal, mine, and unique.

DANCE A SONG

This is the story of a song I want to dance,
I will tell you all in advance,
Between the line of my movements and beyond
I dance the song so fond.

It is the story of the wind
Blowing soft or strong, always the wind,
And me, dancer of the soul with pride
Dancing for the crowd side by side.

Dance and sun warm my body like a balm
Song and music playing like a psalm,
My expression of love and passion
Comes like invocation.

That was the time to have
The existence and the essence to weave,
I have danced on the grass
Everyone saw me pass.

With glory my art got perfection
As I smiled to the crowd ovation,
They were gone and I kept the joy of dancing,
The wind soft or strong always coming.

THE WILL

I swear
For all the jewelry I wear,
The will was written with generosity,
Goods of all variety.

For a long time in the past
I was the favorite and the last,
The only family member,
My aunt's great admirer.

Believe me, nothing was given in vain
I feel so much appreciation,
I love the goods with adoration.
In the past they were shone
Now the shine is gone.

I will polish them with pride
They will be like new I betide,
I have looked at all the pieces so old
And I remember my aunt serving soup, it was col
They now belong to me, it is written in the will,
And I have all of them still.

WHEN THE ONES I LOVE
ARE FOREVER GONE

When the ones I love are forever gone
And the house is alone,
I feel I am not any more
The one I was before.

It is something that changes inside,
I need to heal and learn how to survive,
Crying for the past for days,
I need to heal my pain in many ways.

They were here but not forever
That was a special summer, it will never...
They live now in a clear world with no tomorrows,
It is a far place without sorrows.

Perhaps I will find deep
Resignation for their eternal sleep,
And maybe I will wake up one day
With no tears as I start to pray.

I will change like the seasons' moon
Without the ones I love, without the bloom,
It will be a painful feeling
As I start my own healing.

A WISH FOR PEACE

The story began
In a silent place, plenty of green,
It happened in a dale
Where I learned about the tale.

The day of the commemoration
Brought to me some reflections,
I walked reading names
Without hiding the shame.

They obey the behest
They were fed with pain,
They pursued their true
To end up in the ground.

They got just misery
And a world weeping bitterly,
Suffering sorrow on sorrow
At the graves of that green place.

They deserve the best tribute,
Admiration and a salute
From all the religions in the world.
A wish for peace
For this our world.
A wish for peace
In the deepness of stellar space.

MY HEROES

I understand a hero is someone dear,
The person who in need is near,
And near for me were my family
So my heroes were my parents, specially.

If from a health problem I suffer
And the healing doesn't come from wonder,
My hero is my doctor, who will recover me with pride
And the best care my doctor can provide.

If I need training, my heroes are my teachers,
They spend their life teaching us and no others,
From my teachers I learned the truth
And with pride I succeeded through.

If I need advice,
My hero is my best friend without price,
I can tell you, the heroes I praise
And please don't be surprised,
To choose with intelligence it is all about
Without having any doubt.
So beware for what you choose and need
If you want a life filled with love indeed.

A SONG OF LOVE

A song of love I will sing
For you early this morning,
A song of love in May
In a warm happy day.

With all my feelings I will be singing
And you will love listening,
A sweet guitar playing
And a chorus of friends accompanying.

As soon as the music begins
I am sure your love I will win,
For my deep passionate song I stand
With verses from my land.

This is honest love with no fraud,
The only kind of love I have been allowed,
For you I will be fair,
I promise to be debonair.

Let me treat you with caresses
And offer you these roses,
This is love indeed,
It is pure, whole love, as you believed.

THE PLAY

The main role will be played by the leading man
Young students getting ready as soon as they can,
The music started with a lyric sound
Dancers, artists, and musicians running around.

The theater has a lot of tradition
You can be chosen without condition,
The play was ingenious and clever
And needed the artist to be the best player.

The play talks about marriage,
The whole family can enjoy it at any age,
The author's play has a great personality
The play will be chosen for posterity.

Creation and distinction
The play won merit and consideration,
The author got wealth and position
He became famous with high qualification.

The day of the opening with pride
Everybody was ready and anxious inside,
It was a success by definition
The press gave the play the best reception.

ESSENSE

The season between summer and winter
When leaves turn gold.
The years gone,
The garden, the colors,
The painting on my wall.
Devotion and time,
The sense of power
Side by side the lines of life,
The acknowledgment of existence,
Temper and manners
The strong feeling of desire.
Achieving aims and
The highest values.
The given and the kindness,
Will light up the path.

THE ARTIST

Painting his feelings from within,
With all the fervor an artist can contain,
Visiting landscapes with shores,
Mountains and heavens he explores.

Frozen cold winter with snowground,
Or warm summer all year around,
Bright green bushes,
Symphony of colors from his brushes.

His inspiration is a source naturally,
Something that comes magically,
He rises beyond eternity
And entices with intensity.

The desire is for sure
His expression total and pure,
Beyond words he will stay
Painting on his canvas every day.

He portrayed celebrities very famous,
His art is deep and glorious,
Just a wonder of imagination,
A light blooming with passion.

THE CHINESE DANCER

At the opening, I was an enchanted being
A red and black dancer, I felt like flying,
An ancient gong I heard strong
While a dragon appeared, but not for long.

My silk dress sparkling light
And the crowd smiled with delight,
I waved my multicolored fan with dedication
Moving with grace, and inspiration.

In time came plenty of excellence
To my God Buddha, I greeted with reverence,
My spirit ready to honor in deep
The eternal power to keep.

The close approached soon
The Nirvana I danced boon,
Great stage of gold and crystal decoration,
Sublime music from the land of fascination.

THE PASSAGE

There is a passage between life and death,
The same between light and shadow.

In that passage life abandons you,
In that passage time continues in celestial life.

Which is no life but death,
Which is no death but essence.

The same essence you started,
Before you came to life.

THE PREACHER

He dedicates his life to preach
All over and as far as he can reach.

People listen to him with attention
They say he is the best of the nation.

This is the way of subsistence
He would choose without any doubt in an instant.

Every day a new line of grace
Every day he will arise.

Sometimes people sing or burst into tears,
The preacher shares his feelings with prayers.

THE RETURN

The distant scene from the bridge,
The special beauty of the landscape.

The rigid figures of the shores,
The basic color of the stage.

The whole anthology
Of my past years.

Patterns of my life,
The magic of light.

My house, the view,
The road, and my tears.

The change of the seasons,
The spring and the freshness.

Harmony of composition,
Depth of reflections.

Personal feelings,
My private liasons.

REMEMBER ME

Remember me
When you look at a clear sky.
Remember me
With calm and no desperation,
With a smile and no tears.
When poppies bloom in a field
In warm summer days,
Resting under the trees' fresh shadow.
When you hear the music
I loved so much.
When you see my favorite fruits,
My flowers and my plants
Growing with blossom
In the yard of my house.
When you look at the eyes
Of someone, and theirs remind you of mine.
And remember me for being,
The one I was.

A MUSEUM VISIT

The winter was mild,
The invitation so kind.
I visited the museum that day
To enjoy as long as I could stay.

There were plenty of designs
To appreciate the perfect lines,
A painting of a pilgrimage
Men and women of courage.

A painting of the snow,
People singing a Christmas song in a show,
A painting of the past,
A king, maybe the last.

A painting of a cave,
Cavemen very brave,
A painting about space,
All about the human race.

All of a sudden the dame
In a picture showing her name,
She gave as a donation the ground
And all the paintings around,
The excellence right on the wall,
I love them all.

HEALING FLOWERS IN POWER

With healing power they grow
I keep them in light and shadow,
They are for our health a blessing
We should appreciate with caring.

They are a wonder for this earth
Since the day of my birth,
My mother used to say
"It is marvelous to have them stay".

If we care for them, for centuries we will enjoy
All their benefits with so much joy.
Treatments have been passed
Through generations and they were loved.

They are sublime
Trying them in need and in time,
Maybe marvelous it will sound
Always something precious comes from the ground.

To heal with flowers is wise
This is what I advise,
Hence the importance of a flower
Since the discovery of its power.

YOU WILL BE THERE

I remember you in each poem I read,
In each page I write.

In each star, when I look at the sky,
In each corner of our home.

Each time I hear Beethoven's 5th,
You will be there in those precious things.

You will be there
In the eternal time of tomorrow.

THE POET

I am the one who writes poems,
Inspiration comes sitting beneath the elms,
Finding the right words with clarity,
I write about life, love, and myself, with simplicity.

Imagine the metaphoric space,
And you flying in a dream with grace,
Or waltzing like a dancer
With the excellence of a performer.

My lyrical verse reflected in phases,
My changing vitality and tastes,
Original substantial poems subjected,
Old and new verses are consented.

And still more, they may
Choose verses and gather that day,
When melancholy filled the room,
As I read my poem about the moon.

For my verses I stand cheerily,
They will love them merrily,
I will return in my poems from the past,
Like an enchanted summer they will pass.

THE HOUSE IN FRONT OF MINE

The house in front of mine
Where important names
Were born.
The aged walls
In ecru color,
The brown roof,
The cypress
In the front yard
And the elms in the backyard.
Visited and festered
They stood in line
Waiting to honor
The old famous house
With rooms blossoming in light.
A generation gone
And books, talks, and stories
About their lives ,
Crowded my street.
Seasons passed and the house
Became an old picture
In front of mine.

LOVE, THE PERFECT MEDICINE

I am going to live
Enjoying the love I can give,
With love I can heal in time
Nurturing myself in prime.

Among the ones who share,
We will find a place for us there,
It is a pleasure to delight
Having the love from the ones you invite.

From shore to shore
The news will run soon, far and more.
With love you can survive,
And keep yourself alive.

Without anything to complain,
Love can restore you from pain,
Between earth and heaven you go alone,
Love is the way to be strong.

NATURAL HEALING

" I want a way to heal naturally,"
A friend told me worried sincerely.
I told her that acupuncture and whole herbs,
Are sciences which benefits she deserves.

Acupuncture comes from an ancient land
With millenary sand,
Herbs are natural and pure
And the healing I assure.

WINTER DAY

Winter day at my window,
The wind chills the town,
Snow pilling up on the ground,
The birds flying to another sky.

People come and go, hurry up!
The sun hidden behind the mountains,
Me writing on silk paper,
Sunlight yellow snow
At the top of the hills.

The wind behaves strong,
I pray it does not last too long,
All became clear,
It comes the cold,
The moist still there,
All along the grass.

I looked at the houses in blue,
I saw the white tops of the trees,
The perpetual snow waiting,
As the morning begins,
Winter day at my window.

THEN IMAGINE

You, flying an intense blue sky.

You, messenger of hope, happiness, and beauty.

You, perfect like an original.

You, owner of the space.

You, as the word healer, going across the oceans.

You, enjoying the rainbow's shades,
Gently touching a field of lavender and lilies.

Your sense and generosity,
Will reach the highest, then imagine.

THE CONCERT

The music cherishes my ears
It was the perfect place,
Me devoted to the master's plays
Bach's beautiful suites.

The music intense, magical, divine.
The picturing of freedom,
Reminds me of waves in the sea
Shifting into a new one like a dream.

In the deep the violins sound
Like bees in a whirl dance,
The vitality of the rhythms,
A superb performance.

The impeccable style
Renewed my spirit with splendor,
While the immortal and lovely music
Filled my whole being.

As a prelude for a standing ovation,
I burst into tears almost in silence,
Turning my emotions
Into a healing expression of pleasure.

ONE DAY I WILL BE

One day I will be
The strength of your spirit.

One day I will be
The rain watering your land.

One day I will be
Eternal like remembrance.

One day I will be
All those things and much more.

THE TENDER BREAD

I just the beauty see
As my life perfect can be.

But in love I have been
As clearly you have seen.

It is coming, Spring
With all the peace it can bring.

In glorious shape my roses spread
With tender care I place the bread.

I kneaded it with the purest whole wheat
Now please, it is ready to eat.

MY MOTHER'S CAKES

The music I like to hear,
The perfect time for tea and cake.
They were my best days,
Those days when I enjoyed
The beauty of a table, plenty
Of exquisite pleasures.
I invite you to join me,
Share my bread, my cake,
My table, my tea.
Palate the tasty sweets,
The crust, fresh, superb
And so delicious that we
Can call it divine.
Walk with me the golden way
And come to see my house,
The house of roses and fruits,
Eggs from heavens,
Tender pears, and trees in bloom.
The juice my joy, sweet
From the beginning to the end.
How fondly I vividly remember
My mother's cakes.

THE ROSE

A rose at my window,
Dew in its petals,
Beauty and perfection in color,
Painted or real,
Contemplate the rose with pleasure.
Glorified by inspiration,
Love it unto its petals dry and fall,
Love it for its splendor,
Let it grow with freedom,
Fancy and curled.
Its perfume will involve you
Like an elixir,
Its graciousness,
Its elegance will enchant you.
Rose of my days with magic scent,
Delight and creation.

MY BIRTHDAY

A year more of
Souvenirs to store,
Waiting with expectation
My birthday is a day of celebration.

My mother with devotion used to bake
My favorite delicious cake,
Family and friends gathered around the table,
And we played and talked as much as we were able.

I am fortunate, I have family and so many friends,
With the invitation everybody attends.
The party was a sweet creation
And every year had an innovation.

Having nothing for which to complain,
That day was the best I can explain,
Presents, sweets, and love for everybody who came,
It was a real treat at home.

All my happy birthdays remembered with delight,
They were days of celebration, morning, evening, and night,
Days of flowers, dance, and songs appear,
My birthday is always the best day of the year.

THE ALBUM

The album brings me back images,
They are images from the past,
They belong to a precious time,
That amazingly passed so fast.

Photos from days of laughter and crying
Suddenly wake up my feelings again,
The same I had a long time ago,
The time and its biological laws.

The album that brings me back memories,
The joy, the music and the people I love,
The ones still there
The others that will never be.

Cycles to accomplish,
The capacity to accept,
And my mother, my grandmother,
My great-grandmother, and nothing like us.

Every life there,
The album keeps them all
Beyond subsistence,
Like a constellation.

COMING Of AGE

Coming of age is getting older,
If you live with wisdom you will become wiser.
What counts all above,
In real life is love.

How melancholy, it is
To listen to the past symphonies,
Enjoying them as they rise,
From the past, I praise.

Maybe it is all about lifestyle
What keeps yourself young meanwhile,
You expect years become in gold
It is what waits and holds.

By the time you wake up,
Your time is up,
It is gone the youth,
You will enjoy a warm broth.

A third age to live it is still tender,
So, feel happy it is all about a number.
It is life with a new breeze,
For that you should be pleased.

THE PORTRAIT

It reminds me my best days,
The passion, my youth, my ways.
The portrait on the shelf,
Is a wonder image of myself.

Now that life is gone,
I am going to be like stone.
I am trying to enjoy the treasures,
From the old days of pleasures.

I spend my life praying,
And immense love carrying.
Here and there I delight my friends,
I had to start so many times, as I had so many ends.

All came so intense as before,
The desire, the values, the power and much more.
I propose a pure generous given,
And the blessing will come from heaven.

The portrait I love and keep
Is a fragment of my life I weep,
I want to reach as high as ever
When I will be gone forever.

Copyright, 1996
"The Portrait" first appeared in the anthology
"Tracing Shadows" and in the audio tape
"The sound of Poetry", published by The National
Library of Poetry.

THE PHILOSOPHER

He was fairly well understood,
He was a genius and for his dogmas he stood,
His principles in consideration
Came from his genuine education.

"A philosopher" he stated,
"Is a lover of wisdom,
A friend of freedom".
He was reliant on his own feelings
Explaining the roots of the things.

When he began his exploration,
He reached an accepted conclusion,
He defied scientific explanations,
He was willing to answer questions.

He attributed existence
To the result of substance.
He was a philosopher filled with all humanity,
Willing to defend his doctrines with dignity.

THE COLOR OF THE WIND

The color of the wind,
It is a transparent color,
It comes,
It blows,
It goes,
It touches the blue,
It touches the green,
It kisses my flowers,
It dries my tears away,
It moistens my flowers
Refreshing them all,
With a breeze
Soft and kind,
Sometimes cold
Sometimes warm,
With a breeze
Gentle and idyllic,
With honey smell
And sense of pleasure.

THE STATUE

Royal, symbolic just a creation,
A piece of art beyond conception,
To a young artist entrusted,
Who was chosen for being devoted.

The statue represents history,
The observation is necessary,
To take into consideration
The grandeur and rich condition.

It was the best invitation,
To discover the statue in completion,
What a pleasure to enjoy the collection,
In that original extension.

The specific facilities
Were given with priorities,
The statue has the place,
In the best honorable space.

The artist's decisive work and exposure,
Perfectly suited in sculpture,
The statue was the acquisition,
The artist's proud presentation.

ADIOS MAMA

It happened long ago,
Since then I come to weep
Over her name
Written upon the stone.
This is the way we immortalize,
The carnations give the color,
Green grass grows all around.
Me trying relief to find,
From that enormous pain.
Everyone walking the narrow path
Crying in vain.
The time passes
In the same solitude.
The wind is singing
Between the trees
And my mother is remembered.
Kissing her golden photo,
My tears running I feel,
I am going away as always with a prayer.

MY FAVORITE STAR

You are a far place,
A challenge I have to face,
To reach you one day
And start a road on my way.

Every night you light,
You are beauty to my sight,
With you my secrets I share
And always for me you will care.

THE ACTRESS

She was a celebrity
With a great personality,
She was pure charming expression
Playing roles with dedication.

She knew how to express
Her performance a total success,
The day of the interview,
Everybody took from her a real view.

Clad in a dress sleeved
Very elegant and flowered,
With a rose in sateen white
She talked to the press polite.

It was her real clue
To tell always the truth,
She won acting honors
And gave money as a donor.

When she died, the place was crowded,
She was intensively adored,
With a wealth of appreciation,
Her image will be kept with admiration.

SHARING WITH NATURE

The water and the land
The sun shinning soft,
Birds flying above my home
And across the sky.
The green plants are my food
My mornings and evenings
With my trees in my garden,
And flowers in the whole surface
Of my front and my back yard,
Were pleasing my eyes
And filling my soul with gratitude.
It is a gift from nature,
Please accept this blessing,
And eat from any tree of my garden,
And enjoy the season's fruits.
The produce is tasty
And the water clear,
And there is an altar
Built with stones
At the top of the mountain for you,
To meditate, look at heaven,
And thanks to your God.

REMEMBRANCES

If one day you come back
And I am not here,
Then try to find me
And you will find me,
In the colors of a clear day,
In the singing of the birds,
In the whisper of the wind,
And all will talk to you about me.
I would like to be transparent like water,
I would like to be a bird and flying high,
I would like to be a star and light the night,
I would like to be an artist,
And sing songs for your soul,
I would like to be a plant in the desert,
And survive the solitude and the silence.
I would like to be hard as a rock
And keep my tears forever.

THE CLASS

The class,
The sun coming through the window,
Shadows and light on the wall.

My teacher,
Dedication and time,
The desk her work.

My friends writing poems,
Me writing about them
Me writing about myself.

COLOR ME

Color me with sensibility
And warmth by nature.
Color me with generosity
And as perfect as I would like to be.
Color me loving and kind,
Dear and divine,
Like a Goddess in her kingdom.
Color me with passion
In a landscape with roses,
In a soft light,
When the sun is rising.
Color me in summer,
Rich in harmony
When the air smells
Of fruits and flowers,
And my ocean window
Is plenty of blue, yellow, and orange
Color me with a bead of crystals,
Under a sky fed with stars.
Praise me and love me
Without possessing me,
Like if everything was invented just for us.

EVOCATION TO MY DEAREST

Sorrow is an expression
In time of evocation.

To experience a personal
Grief simply and emotional.

Life and death lie between past and present
Surrounded by community and flowers' scent.

The road was in silence,
Lonely from the distance.

You will be gone for long,
I will sing for you a song.

THE WISH 1

SUN OF THE SEASONS

WARM MY LIFE DAYS,

DON'T LET ME DIE LIKE A NUMBER

KEEP ME ALIVE FOR THE WONDER.

THE WISH 2

I WANT ETERNAL LIFE,

TO ENJOY FOREVER

THE JOY OF BEING ALIVE.

THANKS, MAMA

Thanks for being there always for me.

Thanks for dedicating your life to all of us.

Thanks for teaching me every day.

Thanks for helping me always in a good way.

Thanks for early years filled with happiness.

Thanks for being the way you were.

Thanks for your love and understanding.

Thanks today and always.

WEDDING

Sun of my universe
For you is my verse.

I imagine summer
And you my unique lover.

You and me the waltz dancing,
Everybody happiness wishing.

My faith in love
For you I will prove.

Tomorrow together
God will join us forever.

THE EMIGRANT

The work on the island was a hard allure
To emigrate on a new road for sure,
I knew if I tried a new place
I would have challenges to face.

Early the peasants started the walk,
I joined them to work, silent, I didn't talk.
That evening I spoke about my decision in form,
In my home the news was like a storm.

I sat on a chair by the window surely
Trying to keep back my tears purely,
So willing with courage I behave,
I felt happy for being brave.

After that was a calm all around
With a soft music as a sound,
I felt it was mine the world wide
And my sorrow I put aside.

I promised my family from me they would learn
To visit each year I will return,
It was a hot June silent day
The day I went away.

WRITING POEMS IN THE CLASS

It took for me some time,
The inspiration came with the first line,
Once I started I had the rhythm
I crafted my poem like a hymn.

I wrote with dedication
Patience and inspiration,
It is all that you need
To write a poem indeed.

DAYS OF YOUTH

The warm wind soft and gentle,
The joy of being in college,
Reminiscences of glorious days.
The sunlight orange and red
The past years are linking
At the end the celebration
With new photos for the collection.
The walls of my college
In pink and beige color,
The silence in the air
The day was gone.
The refined decoration
Respected in all its beauty,
The college was a pictorial adventure.
Tomorrow a new clear day
With warm wind
Will come back again.

I NEED

◆ I need justice to rule the world and devotion to peace to be the best of all religions.

◆ I need a good world built with knowledge, goodness, courage and a free intelligence.

◆ I need a world with hope and a future, where individuals can determine the kind of life they wish to lead.

◆ I need the triumph of life over tragedy and true intelligence to pursue happiness.

◆ I need goodness and honesty as human values.

◆ I need people filling their own story with love.

QUOTATIONS

By Delia B. Freinquel

- Success is to achieve the most important accomplishment with yourself.

- To set values for your life is one of the most important things you can do for yourself.

- To be healthy means to have energy, optimism, and confidence.

- Tradition is the celebration of the past for the future generation.

- Self-confidence and freedom are the best fortunes you can have.

- Love and understanding are the best medicine.

- The essential source of creativity is inside you, if you believe in yourself.

- I am conscious of my own mortality, but in my inside world, life seems to be forever.

- When we have to make important decisions and face special situations, it is important to look into our own soul.

- Creativity is the road to freedom.

- Your decisions are always the beginning of something important.

- Be sensitive to the needs of others.

- You find what you need inside yourself.

- The truth will be always at the end of the path.

- Work for your happiness because none will do it for you.

- Happiness is a precious time that passes amazingly fast.

- Years may take beauty away, but years add beauty into our life and into our way with more wisdom every day.

- Simplicity is the key of happiness.

- If you are inspired by great ideals you will have a generous view of the world.

- Always be a winner, because to be a winner is in your mind.

- To observe and participate are two principles needed to get along with life.

- Loneliness lets you go deep into yourself.

- Private affections have an important role in our public attitude.

- Our beliefs are our own doctrines.

- Legacy should be one of the most important issues for all human beings.

- Our rich personal and symbolic language is the one which reflects our emotions.

- We need to learn to free our feelings and our beliefs like a religion.

- Sometimes the truth is designed by ourselves for our own benefit.

- Well-being in life is a state of the soul where balance plays the essential role.

- Love is our spiritual food.

- Things are easier when you feel gratitude.

- To have wellness means to have patience, toleration, sensitivity, and caring.

- Take the line of dignity instead of the line of indignation.

- Healing words sometimes have more power than medicine.

- The existence and future of the human race depends on the capacity of each individual to perform with excellence essential functions.

- To accept the truth is to accept things with honesty.

This book is dedicated
to the memory of my
mother Jacinta and to
all my readers.